skeptical erections

skeptical erections

mxolisi dolla sapeta

2019© Mxolisi Dolla Sapeta
All rights reserved

ISBN: 978-0-9947104-4-4
ebook ISBN: 978-0-9947104-5-1

Deep South
contact@deepsouth.co.za
www.deepsouth.co.za

Distributed in South Africa by
University of KwaZulu-Natal Press
www.ukznpress.co.za

Distributed worldwide by
African Books Collective
PO Box 721, Oxford, OX1 9EN, UK
www.africanbookscollective.com/publishers/deep-south

Earlier versions of some of these poems were published in
Tyhini 2016 (ISEA, Grahamstown), and *New Coin*

Cover design: Liz Gowans and Robert Berold
Text design and layout: Liz Gowans
Cover painting: Mxolisi Dolla Sapeta, *Echoes 3*

contents

I

II

bottom of an envelope

i always measure you when you sleep
and borrow your sorrows
between a jacket
and a pocket deep with glass scrapers

i have a bullet of a mind
lost in the pace of a wild horse
that gallops the fringes
of joza, gugs, new bright and soweto

please forgive my apologetic speech and reason
for my brains are battered
by the van wyks, van der merwes and maybe you
for a double reason locked at the bottom of an envelope

every day i wear judgment on my way to work
at the home affairs department
where i am found dancing inside a gumboot
flooded by the blankness of my conscience

and remain armed with nothingness
i stink that too

peace

i always dream of being dangerous
feared by everyone
the children especially
stop their nagging for everything
money for the fucking sweets
with just one blank merciless glance
i get to sleep peacefully
dream of being dangerous again

township

the township is a suspicious place
it never stops to snitch and guzzle
it never forgives and learns
i am a talking township
i rise and fall where the township falls
i have a colossal share in its fatherless children
and ownerless dogs in the barking streets

my town
for port elizabeth

i want to lose this disappointed town
with a broken face that stands for everything rotten
a forgery with no soul on its way to oblivion
an intruder with no logic proportion
with no colour of conscience or even a muted reason
an incomplete image shaped out of a twisted existence
its eyes remain to resemble dishonour
its gateways perverse out of self-inflicted deceits
it stumbles with a hypocritical modesty
i am unable to make up an apologetic mockup
with words formed out of loathing
so distorted that i echo direct from its glare
without any depth to retreat to
why not try this highway leading to the red light district
for it has a fair path of sales beneath our reason

discordant flags

houses speak a random emptiness
the streets face a veil of discordant flags
in front of doors sealed with a rigid silence
remote memories blink without a sound
a fat policeman is watching through his big sunglasses
and a shining revolver
while a slow fly dangles the nostrils of a ticking age

beyond rooftops

there is this cadmium stink of meat
maybe red –
followed by cerulean winds
of a muddled sky smoke
pulling under a turquoise-grey cityscape
with scattered regrets of installations
finally converging
towards a foreground of high values
staring at a vanishing point
of washing lines and lamp posts
accident of a stark colourfield
too bright with all the wrong colours
behind this is a crimson heaven
always waiting

rain poem

the rain stands alone on a night
where it shuts your door with a thunder
a lightning for the bachelor
and many drops for a bird
it will run for a gutter
drum for the roof
it will drench on a poor soul
passing through with no one to go to
but don't wait
random porches won't shelter strangers
on drizzling nights like this

the gate

i wanted to run away wholeheartedly
but kept coming back to my falling gate
decorated with thorns and worms
as people watched wishing it could fall on my feet
i had to fix it with my twisted hands
for queens and whores kept it squealing and screeching
banging at the rotten door with their heavy wet breasts
they would come out with a wig under one armpit
and looking for the other shoe

city

the city does not end
on a night like this
stillness nibbles at the nippy stench
from men without tongues
inside of unmarked graves
slam a door down the throats
of greedy loiters from frustrated prostitutes

whispers from gloomy cars pass the time
i make my own glory in this solitary hour
on this bed and in your frail sweaty arms
i am the smell of warm colours that glow
the long night of mutinies
i am the wood that burns its history in this siren forest
and i am still here, you too

you and you and you

behind those austere bookshelves
your warped hips keep me peeping through words
passing you is always suicidal with intermittent slides
of a one-minute fine love affair
right here in front of you and i die again
no one notices
i wake to your visually assaulting body
your breasts dangling in my brain
and i die unnoticed deaths
under those trees and pedestrian crossings
filled with voluptuously throbbing bodies
that never look my way

and by all means

your bosom is my heaven and i remain your pilgrim
i falter deep in your long gloomy passage
i am aware of its persuasive enormity
i worship all the stretching hours fading there
because you have dark places in you
dragging me to the murky wetness of your body

where you always rise

i eat my liver at three o'clock every night
under a flimsy lantern
and i keep falling and falling
on a thick glorious grime
with spontaneous frictions
i blink apologetically
toward the corner of the street
where you always rise
with twists of a vulgar shape
a stabbing glance
i grip at your slippery heartbeat
with a bloated thirst
and babble my ways into your shadow
my brain must have been foggy
to have remained taut in your crucifix
but to this day
it has inhabited a place
across the street where you always rise

ordinary songs

the songs you wrote
had cushioned nipples and warm belly buttons

the songs i wrote
were alone on a cold battle mountain

the night you left me drunk
under foggy erections of lamp posts
frozen –

you swallowed a fire heaving swollen pubic moons

your night

the night has a muffled sound
a sleeping shadow
it travels swiftly through vast planes
untouched –
and through enormous hearts
of babies lying on crumpled pillows

i am your night sometimes
i have a sky and many stars for you
but please remember
the night has massive secrets
and tales about lost men
it whispers their names
the wind – the planes – the stars

sshhh listen...
i am here behind you

all men

i said to the barman wear me out
and give me another
the door creaked open as she finally walked in
right when my liver started to rot
her footsteps ground a shrill deep in my wallet
where i violate my gloom
every morning at about four o'clock
running away from the loud snoring of her pussy
and its endless spout of dead semen
scented with cheap alcohol
long after the rants and screams
of the vulgarity she carries in her pouch
her fingernails marked vigorous trails
that covered my body like a street tattoo
and I wane under the thunder of her footsteps

on women

there is music of birds in your eyes
delights jiggle your bloods, pledge the earth
it marks a painful circle inside your gut
honey is a snitch between your legs
make your own tribe pith of genius

mahoti

gliding through the blue wind with a hiss
his troubles are mounting his waist
with acid wings and blows
they take him to the middle of a field
a goat browbeats
when rumours gather a child's heart
we know
they bury him in a window

anger

each sermon ends like a fixed triumph
the boys are balding behind gloomy suits
and rows of dirty benches
the sultry sun will accompany them home
inside their stomach is the staunch aloofness
that disperses the clutter in street corners –
it does not recognize the faces of men who
weep and gather there; it despises their truths because
they smear their anger aloud on the public eye.
when they finally reach their own homes
rooted in empty bowels and kitchens
the anger whistles a slow song; crawls out of their pockets
and spreads itself on a man's forehead
he silently throws his suit at the feet of a widow
who waits across the street

condition 1

child is with child on her back
scraping and shuffling through government grants
the money goes as far as the barbed-wire spaza shop that never ends
the streets are jam-packed and never forgive
choruses of barking from ownerless dogs
random gunshots and the alarming growth of shebeens,
mini-malls, churches and beauty salon containers
the rich motherfucker with rows of fat layered thick neck
the malnourished habitual car guard who watches your car
whether you leave it attended or not
the sexy waitress who almost forgets to pick your bill if you are black
and the endless letters in your postbox that keep reminding you
to pay your tv licence

fatherland

little devils heave in furious settlements
crash behind the same dialect of old fashioned freedoms
narrowed by isms that exist in repetitive ideals of their absence
heaps of hollow songs are buried inside their own fixations
and the looting continues

second death

slam down your spirit comrade
there will be no announcements on your second death
a speech will be delivered through the shrill of a fat bird
and we won't have an audience this time

dreams and heroes

each day I am repeatedly told that it's ok, that I am truly part of a harmony. the next day I am erased and promised to be redefined with detailed contours. my name and colour remains in a pile of papers in that austere corridor, a long one, when our names remain hidden in rapid graves and their memories dismissed. i know we won't have a proper war or monuments like other places. our dreams and heroes will be for sale as disposable statues in the city storefronts.

every word

i have heard words too many
about the horrors and filth
of poking one's vigour in countless ovens
all these words coming alive in my ears
through lofty door gaps and echoed hallways
mother to father – mother to uncle
and when my time came i stood in the middle of things
with a cavernous deaf flirt
all i could hear was my father's drunken whisper
to the cleaning lady – to the neighbor's daughter – to the postwoman
uncle's constant brag about his size and stamina
words too many
in streets full of breathing ovens
behind every word
uncle's voice – father's drunken whisper – mother's unforgiving back

violent seed

i am from a violent seed – a legacy of vulgarity
a suitcase packed with stones and bullets
across the railway line things may seem different
but on tv and in the neighbourhood temper is boiling

every night i dream of a violent childhood
an unfair love from both my parents
now deceased – left no money of course
my father casts a fearsome shadow behind all my mirages
his tongue still blocks my ears with a sharp trill
my mother's voice was soothing though she never smiled

I never mock the drunken anger in my neighbourhood
it's the wine we drank on fridays that made us happy
the girls made us happy too
they also gave us children we never wanted or trusted
love was a mysterious nagging word we did not know
and i never managed to say
this is my house!
the heroic words my father used when he was drunk
there was always something suspicious about happy people
everybody's weapon was a fierce temper

on new year's day in the beachfront
people look poor but fat
and the colour of the grass is a bleached fawn
the whites are stubbornly holding onto their pompous standards
holding hands together – ice cream cones with hopeless hands
they are becoming redder than a yellow-white
their smiles have missing teeth and truths
their eyes are a glassy cold blue
like the unforgiving ocean shores

i could not even find a tiniest lime light from my girlfriend
she had long disappeared behind the screens of soap operas
and the makeshift beauty salon containers jammed in street corners
to ease the constant pain of being a black woman
in an unimportant township somewhere in africa
her only weapon was a borrowed beauty,
a sexy body, and the endless fashion trends from china

sunflower

an abrupt midget pees on a sunflower
shake his penis rigorously with a fat hand
turns his head from left to right
spats with a heavy thud on the wet ground
the moon carries a doubtful glare
walks away like a man who wears the night

condition 2

i wake up all pouring last night's alcohol sweat, my bones crack inferiority timbres. i go and take a leak in the dim silence. after gulping down a glass of tap water i lay my head for a while. i can feel that I am going to puke so i sneak back to the loo, vomit already aggressive towards the mouth. i gag and keep going – kneel and let it all out. white stuff like foam.

i fantasize that a woman with a jug of water is standing behind me, massaging me all over my shoulders and asking me to let it all out again and again. i gargle and return to sleep, headache pounding perspiration of torments. i manage to lie my head on the damp pillow. i don't care if it rains storm or a morning ocean – it is morning, so the light will come.

i start hearing familiar voices from the street. draw the curtains and open the window for fresh air. i see some of the girls from the neighborhood who always come to me for free drinks with icy cold ciders and food parcels, they slowly stroll down the street tossing their buttocks individually from one side to the other. they look fit enough to drink for the next ten years.
i go back to my mattress and close my eyes and within time a six-pound hammer thunders against the cement wall above my head – my neighbour's constant work on his property.

back yard melodies

they fill their entrances with drenched blades
flags waving like welcoming gaudy
the butcher boys are baking anxious melodies
with high pitched tones in the back yard
two hearts are suspended with an electric cord
from the porch ceiling – pumping and clogging
one belongs to an unknown animal and the other
to a newborn baby the size of a bullet hole

poets

this poet wears a mask made with tinsel of the american dream
a smoking cannon anticipates his orders at the peak of his
                                                    twitchy fingers
he regrets our hungers here
washes his salmon down with suave wines and wastes himself
in perfumed pussies in room 404
he quietly lays automatic rifles and heaps of speeches
under the pitiful shade of the sudanese poet
and waits for a world war to flatten canada since there are no old
                                                    men there
the pages of the book he reads are separated by razor sharp
                                                    bayonets

condition 3

the sun begins to crack through the holes of the window – i
jump up and rush down to buy painkillers and swallow all the
pills right in front of this dirty goggle-eyed shopkeeper. i walk
back home without looking at him. a sandy-coloured stray dog
gallops next to me all the way back. it limps here and there
through the murky fragments of the morning mist. it carries a
rotten half-moon shaped wound revealing a sun-soaked internal
rib cage. some bones are hanging down as it limps tirelessly,
not looking at me. i don't want to confront a direct stare
because i am keeping the spontaneous pace – two women are
conversing over the boundary wall; the one woman slowly gives
the other a funeral obituary.

high kites

it was the kind of night when you fly a kite or watch the stars
all by themselves. the colour of the sky was already high. there
were no cities and flags, just the sky and the wind making
sound against the kite, blowing and bouncing. no windows to
watch the sight from. my eyes were starting to stream tears
from the wind encounter, skating through my vision like steel,
like drops of steel. the kite was free. and the fog murmured:
don't die again.

charlie

this morning when i was looking for a boy to send to the local spaza i saw charlie. he was wearing a bleached cap displaying an alcohol brand, an old clean white shirt, a trouser with no recognisable colour and flip-flops. it's a year since i saw him roaming about the same space. charlie never left white location. he did work for a number of companies as a van-boy, hand lender or assembly line fitter. i was born in white location too and charlie was older than me. his hey-days when he worked the companies and played for the local soccer team and banged a few girls that have now aged too. he still lives in a back room of the house he was born in. i still live in the house i was born in too. i was away for a year, and never thought of charlie. when i came back i heard about a few neighbours who had passed away. i never thought of them either. the little boys i send so often to the spaza have not really grown. they still play soccer in the open playground at the back of my house. i used to play soccer there when i was a little boy too. i still send them to the local spaza. i am welcomed by merry-go-round whispering stories – no hugs – no high fives. no one knows why i was away for a year. all people want to know is when will i be going away again. i never pay attention to gossip but this time i want stories to write, so i listen. after a few hours i want a couple of tea bags and loose cigarettes and go out of the back yard to look for the boys. the boys are still playing soccer in the playground and charlie is sunbathing close to my house together with bra wonder and bra mandi. they are startled when they see me and i go to greet them briefly and call out to the boys who come running to me. they know what i want from them and are looking for the tips i always give. charlie, bra wonder and bra mandi are drinking ship sherry under the sun. the boys return and give me my tea bags and cigarettes. i give them a small tip and go back inside the house leaving the boys to their soccer. bra wonder had the same life experiences as charlie and bra mandi. they were all born in white location and have worked for a few companies in the city and played for the local soccer team and are now old. sometimes bra wonder is happy when he is drunk, or bra mandi. i never saw charlie happy.

windy of port elizabeth

they drink black wine with a shuddering voice behind a city of muted winds. the splinters of its memories hang in the air like crack paradise and the alley walls are smeared with rows of drunk urine. sunbathers of this city praise a vulgar priest who plunges into its infant vagina as long as he adds a lullaby in the word of god. mothers recite his name until they fall dead flat on the hard-on laps of their sons who breathe tik through their hearts like spineless dragons. they rise in the delicate hand of night to whip the streets – their mothers. and the city continues to lumber through a windy end of the universe.

condition 4

for years your deceased father's foot prints are found speckled
we are dazed with anxieties when passing your house these days
the only hope lies in the women's potential to serve in your funeral
there are rumours that your grandmother never dies
between your life and its absence stands the void of your presence
but if you die we will all lose common touch
there will be no more sunbathing behind the walls

sound of my breath

dogs always bark when i cough
and i am constantly annoyed
by the sound of my breath
my loyalty to sadness
that keeps away from happiness
harbouring no space for disappointments
and i wish all music can die

sea child

my wounds are sheltered inside a sea child
her language is buried by a roar
of the wave she carries on her shoulders

she does not open her eyes
towards the trapped earth

her ocean is locked inside a suitcase

1967

i wake inside your hour of the day
if you smoke a pipe on your father's chair
decide what you want to take from my body before I burn
last breaths of lonely souls moisten the air
there's no need to dress up
1967 was a year of the government sugar

always knew

i always knew
about the sharp places in my father's voice
in his tales about the universe
there was always black and white
i viewed them from a stand
not his nor mine

he spoke of death with a troubled voice
a voice as thin as ice
it sharply pierced through the hearts of sick men
lying in hospitals and brothels
he spoke quietly with a shrill

i knew about the broken doors in my father's house
about every wrecked dream
only his face was showing gleaming cracks
from tears that had dried up after years of untold sights
he was a man of many empty voices
i half listened to him as I sucked seasons
from my mother's two-tone breast
her sour milk had dried up through the years
of crying and trying to stop his beatings

and so you say

and so you say
i masturbate in deserted cathedrals
to relieve my haunted hidden conscience
from the anxious eyes of the children

my stand is shaking as a man
i stumble in my dreams
a walking contradiction
self-distracted
i am not to be trusted
i wet my bed in the unforgiving hours

i sleep with tender infants
rejected by their pregnant mothers
who impose their thirst on rich perverts
i protect my weak stand with constant lies
that i was born and raised with a dozen kittens
inside a wooden suitcase
in a cheap motel in southend
that my only toy as a child
was the hairy penis of an alien neighbour
the result of my small brains
a victim for blind sex
in the dark quick alleys of the makeshift neighbourhood
i will die grinning with a fat distorted belly

fiery corridors

father leaves for work every day in the morning
he returns soaked in exhaustion at dusk
hazy black eyes buried in his pale skin
his voice vague, all disfigured out

i mourn mother who just died
before finally leaving her under a long tree
she has been buried behind a heavy curtain
behind a door and the many doors of our house
bedridden for the past seven months
becoming blurred in father's hazy desires

i do not meet father in the grey corridors
in the winter of our five-roomed house
in the seasons of our distance
he had the audacity to bring a sexy wife
just three weeks after mother's death
betraying me to spend all the days listening to her footsteps
through the chill of our narrow corridors
she chases my eye contact everywhere
she fills the house with the odour of her starving pussy

father is drenched under a disappearing industry
always overloaded by the fraudulent church
the place where he met the corrupt-prone sexy mother
i remain behind my bedroom door with a rigid fury
stepmother haunts my flesh – father is no more
no colour
father brings home food and the word of god

i am terrified by stepmother
i spend my days escaping her odour
under the grey shadows of our tacit passages
stepmother gallops through the corridors in her panties
father brings food at dusk – i do not get out of my room
there is no need
i breathe stepmother's odour – i grieve for mother
with the void of father's absence
i falter deep and get accustomed to her odour
i hear the click of the door, father's gone to work

the odour consumes the house, my exile
it confuses my solitude, it confronts father's absence
i start chanting her name behind
the long shadows of my bedroom door
spending all my days sniffing her odour – chasing her trail

i remain open to my bleedings
she wants my blood – i want her odour
the day i tore her flesh apart
she was wearing mother's panties
my mother's odour
behind the curtains that drenched her life away
that day i entered my mother's open grave
wearing a mask decorated with father's absence and an odour
and to this day
i remain on the floor of mother's grave, chanting her name

master

whiteness is always hiding
behind the dark, behind the death
do you want death?
do you want the shadow or do you want blacks?
no i dare not,
everybody wants white because it chases the shadow
it chases the widow and the blacks
my master is white - my teacher is white - my church is white
and i don't want the widow and the shadow and the blacks
master rapes my mother when i sleep
and he gives me food in the morning
i love master!

the morning is always thick; my eyes are thick in the morning
i want to sleep and wait for mother to give me food
and i love the sun and food
i hate the morning because father
always wants to beat me in the morning
i want sun and mother;
mother makes me happy and I eat all the food
master makes me work in the garden
and he beats father behind the field
sometimes master rapes father too, sometimes he rapes me
master is a rapist and he hides behind
the widow and shadow and blacks
but i love master –

i know you want to write a story and i won't allow that
i don't want a story and i don't want all your bad stories
i don't want you to press a button to tell my story because you lie
your teeth make you lie
your eyes make you bad
and your white smile makes you rape everything
my friend will come at night, my friend is the shadow
my friend does not want your bad stories when mother sleeps
but father wants your stories in the night
father is bad too –

father and master are big thieves
and they chase each other when mother sleeps

i see those two big thieves from the window
wearing masks and chasing each other every night
master hates father and father hates master
but they smile when they see mother

father rapes mother too
and he does not give me food like master
i want mother to smother father with her big pie
because father likes mother's big pie
master likes mother's big pie too, she must smother master too,
those two rapist thieves!
but mother loves the two rapists;
she always gives them her big pie and cries in the morning
i love mother –

i always see mother tearing apart,
always in the morning with her tears
i want to wipe them with my bare soul
but father wants to drink the tears and get drunk
father is always drunk and hides his food,
mother cries and gives me food
master never cries or gets drunk or smiles
master speaks like a good man but master has a big gun
he wants to shoot father –
father speaks like a hero but he wants to be like master
i don't want to be like father or master
i want to be like mother but i won't give them my big pie
no! i don't have a big pie like mother,
i won't be raped and cry in the morning
i won't be like mother –

father keeps coming home to hide from master,
master wants father all the time
i hate looking at them from my window –
master leading with a whip in hand
father follows him carrying his own tears in two full bags
father does not drink his own tears
i know when father and master die i will be a good man
but i won't drink my own tears like mother
i think she choked and drowned in her own tears
for master and for father – i won't die like that
i will take master's big gun and shoot him even if he is dead

father too!
i will hunt both of them inside their graves
and kill them again and again
maybe mother can wake then, mother, oh dear mother
i didn't know who to blame,
but i wanted to blame someone for you
i wanted to blame father but i sleep well when i blame master
it was all his fault, the rapes, the tears and the beatings

a man

he brings heap of wrath with his heart
his pockets cannot carry the clout from the metals he digs
below the bleating soil that suffer scarifications each dawn
he buries his bruises and beard there
every day –
and comes home to his children and wife timid and exhausted
does not tamper with dreams anymore
god knows he knew what he knew about the world
muted screams from battered lovers; taste of their blood

he travels to the four-hundred-year old missing dialect
inside the belly of nothingness and rock a chair where the
                                                    rain ends

he continues to buckle his suit higher and tighter
as long as it bears a price tag that shelters his brains
sometimes he dies like everything, like courage or heartbeats
and at the end of each day all he wants is a state funeral
a word from the strange priest who looks like an important man
and when there is nothing left in him
the sun leaves him to the bottom of the soil he has been digging
and the grinding begins to nibble at him until there is nothing
                                                    but the soil

old men

you start running from the houses
naked and all wet
old men breathing after you
battling to grab you
battling with their oldness
you frantically pick up all the stones
claiming the stones are your money
that you must have all the stones
the old men keep dragging you
inside the long shacks
locked for silent perversions
and you lurk by the windows
trying to get out and pick up the stones
sometimes waving for help
you break the windows
the old men gather behind the shadows
of the corrugated iron shacks in your back yard
turned into ruins of rust
all broken with black holes
the wind whispers the old men's names
they stare back at you with slow eyes
carrying their solid tears

homecoming

when they heard you were coming back home
they stood frozen on the edge of the valley
backs tilted against the east – not blinking
they spat one tooth toward the north each year
eyes turning into humid monochromes at dusk
the world kept shifting under their feet
there was something about the hymn they sang
that suggested the wind would pace your homecoming

they decided to kneel before cryptic shadows
and inside of cathedrals, doors were kept closed
silently hoping under candle-lit corridors
they would only rise to sing and blink dry tears of sorrow
all their hopes bottled towards jerusalem
only appearing at dawn in every winter
crossing the sacred lands with hands placed on their heads
not turning –

in their hearts the world was holding your homecoming back
and each day of the waiting –
their bodies were quietly mangled behind the gardens
as mothers kept crying for their sons' premature deaths
with tears drowning the spirit of the world
believing there was everything about every place you travelled
your destiny not known to them
it was hard to believe you were coming home
spending your life preparing for everyone's death

after a while they only gathered to curse the universe
only keeping their shadows visible under the moon
as they have been believing in empty truth
to be broken in the hands of your freedom
and only preferred to admire your beauty
on cursed misty mirrors smeared with human fat

isolated times

buried deep in root trails
of words gone astray
washed up in cattle fields
dead babies' names
will wait under a rock
filled with bones and wood

their loins smothered by a coil
of an ancient hair
inside distant shrines of a missing sea
witches will wear cyclical beats
of a dark heart
chanting the lost rain
hoping the sun will sweep the sin away
with a lifeless sword that never kills
of long gone bearded men
who stood their ground
so the rain will fall
and the grinding of the cosmos that never forgives

blawa

for new brighton

a mixture of odours pour severely inside his half open
kitchen door. nogregre is slushing words between her close
tight tobacco-stained teeth. she struggles to stand steady.
the mouthwatering scent of the chicken soup he cooks is
overpowered by her incident at the door. every time she
opens her mouth he wants to scream whereupon he gives
her whatever money he has in his pockets. all against his will.
she lazily grabs the money and reels her unhappy tarnished
eyes towards him. he pleads for her to leave without saying
another word. her wry smile is left hanging alarmingly on the
endless bottom half of his kitchen door, she staggers away
unconsciously. victoriously dripping sticky breasts out of her
open shirt. and she continues to disappear in the spiteful dust
from the shuffling drunken lot wandering about the streets of
blawa. the sun stands still on everybody's head here – fixed.
their planes are parched and battered. and he knows they will
eat anything between money, whippings and penises. he sits
in the cool shade of his kitchen blinking. trying to regain his
sense of purity after she's gone. the holy surface he constantly
drags from church every sunday. slowly, the scent of the
chicken soup comes back to life in the kitchen air and he starts
breathing faith. he realises that he is actually staring right into
his grandfather's eyes and skips a heartbeat. they remind him
that he was born in this house, in fact it was his grandfather's
house that his father inherited and later he inherited it from
his father. and since childhood he always flinched at this
photograph; made him uneasy. after haphazardly handing over
all his money to the drunken girls passing through; he starts
feeling naked and guilty under the gaze of his grandfather. in
this state of horniness and holiness, he considers removing the
photograph but fights against the thought. he firmly assures
himself that it is just a photograph, nothing less nothing more.
he did not touch these lost girls in that way anyhow. unfortunate
sinners who have nothing but unbearable thirst. he says prayers
after drowning in his own cautious depravations. makes sure
he wraps his grandfather's picture with a clean cloth when he
fiddles in personal intimacies. he is certain that god will provide
a special place of forgiveness for him.

all my killers

I died with a skeptical erection
a grin and a vulgar despair
inside a spontaneous shallow grave
dug by thirsty homeless assholes
with no sense of line, structure or depth
with a tiny bone stuck in my membrane
I remember your glare – your quandary – your crave
thriving through a thousand virus-tainted spinal grooves
and grease-hardened nostrils

I have forgiven all my killers
including these fucking bugs
coming in and out of my remains as they wish
at least my killers from the alleys knew my name
and I remember the days when I could just crush a bug
in the faint shadows of your debt-soaked house
there was always this Steve guy
watching porn clips in the dining room
you never introduced him to me but he was always there

i am sure you have your ways
now that I am gone forever
as you always thought I was drowned in sin
when mother gave the much regrettable birth to me
unplanned –
so if you ask me now, yes I mean now
in the bleakness of my grave hole with these bugs stripping my flesh
i will say go fuck your mother
because I suspect you were a baptized child
while I was dumped with drunkards – random neighbors
and was made to share the kitten's milk on a daily basis
put to sleep with a few stiff tots of cheap liqueur

god's plan

all i had were thoughts about a single heaven in the sky
followed by long rows of questions about women stuck in there
possibly without men to caress their troubled bodies
their swollen breasts and loins silently screaming for a touch
a hard thrust of perspiration drumming and evoking fishy smells
i guess that's what deprivation does to their platonic existence
their nudity without impact or meaning to the holy men

right on this night i lost thoughts of nudity
the many scattered visions of a cousin's blossoming pubis
through the peeping gaps i create in my blanket
and the doors i leave ajar
all lost now in the burdening phase of maturity
and now i deeply yearn to suck all those women in heaven
feel the texture of their nipples with my long thin tongue
gulp their milk until they have nothing but blood
if they still have blood anyway

i want to drip their swollen breasts empty
i dread the dripping but i am all dripping too
my mouth dripping pasty saliva
my pants constantly damp from the dripping of my wiggly hot penis
and the pastor keeps reminding me of hell!
and i know god has a plan for everyone, for every need
and mine is to empty the souls of those women in heaven

unborn

i wake up inside your thick murky intestines
my eyes are struggling to open
your heartbeat is pounding on my brains
seeing and breathing your internal red smells
only when you utter vulgar words
the light flickers through your mouth
and i realise i am wrestling for life
a frightened fetus at the bottom of your gloom

Printed in the United States
By Bookmasters